Suzuki

VIOLA SCHOOL

Volume 6
Viola Part
Revised Edition

AMPV: 1.01

© 1993, 2000 Dr. Shinichi Suzuki

Sole publisher for the entire world except Japan:

Summy-Birchard, Inc.

Exclusive print rights administered by

Alfred Music Publishing Co., Inc.

All rights reserved.   Printed in USA.

ISBN 0-87487-491-2

INTRODUCTION

FOR THE STUDENT: This material is part of the worldwide Suzuki Method® of teaching. The companion recording should be used along with this publication. A piano accompaniment book is also available for this material.

FOR THE TEACHER: In order to be an effective Suzuki teacher, ongoing education is encouraged. Each regional Suzuki association provides teacher development for its membership via conferences, institutes, short-term and long-term programs. In order to remain current, you are encouraged to become a member of your regional Suzuki association, and, if not already included, the International Suzuki Association.

FOR THE PARENT: Credentials are essential for any Suzuki teacher you choose. We recommend you ask your teacher for his or her credentials, especially those related to training in the Suzuki Method®. The Suzuki Method® experience should foster a positive relationship among the teacher, parent and child. Choosing the right teacher is of the utmost importance.

In order to obtain more information about the Suzuki Association in your region, please contact:

International Suzuki Association
www.internationalsuzuki.org

CONTENTS

The compositions in this volume were arranged for viola and piano by Doris Preucil. The viola parts were edited by William and Doris Preucil with the approval of the Suzuki Association of the Americas Viola Committee.

4

Tonalization

S. Suzuki

Tonalization exercises should be practiced at each lesson.
Exercise for beautiful tone and vibrato.

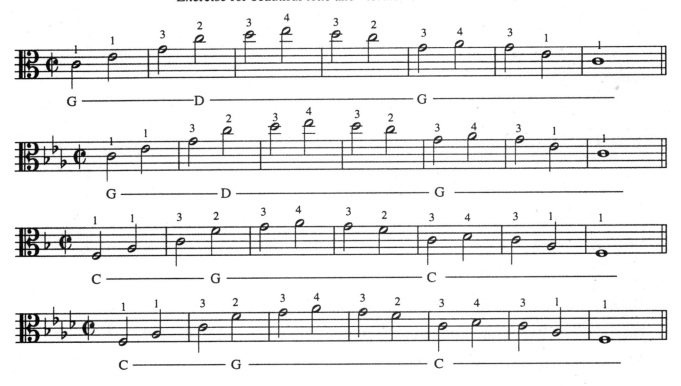

Exercises for finding exact intonation

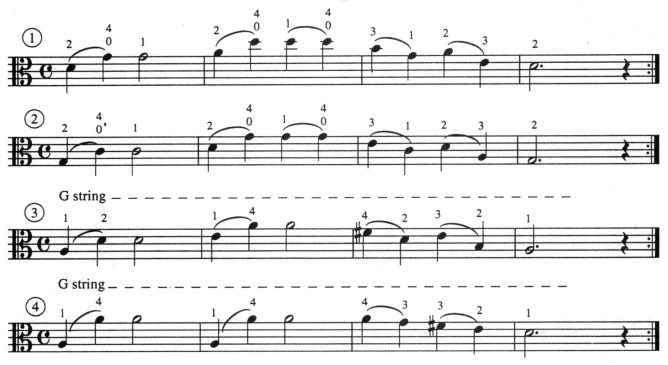

Shifting exercises for #4

Exercises in Octaves

D. Preucil

Also practice #2
with overlap bowing:

Also practice #3
with this variant:

Keep fingers 1 and 4 down
when shifting

Exercises in Sixths

Practice as follows:

1 La Folia

M. Marais
Realized and arranged by Doris Preucil

Allegro moderato (♩ = 76)

VAR.I - Dolce (♩ = 76)

2 Allegro

G.H. Fiocco

Examples of ornaments

written   played

3 Suite in G Major

J.S. Bach

Allemande (♩ = 60)

14

4 Arioso

J.S. Bach

Chromatic Scale Exercises

D. Preucil

First practice slurring one beat. Then practice with one bow for each measure.

Three Octave Scales and Arpeggios in D major and D minor.

Use full bows with smooth bow and string changes.

D. Preucil

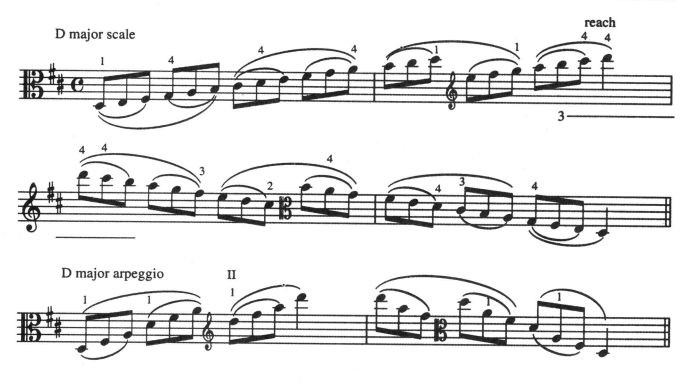

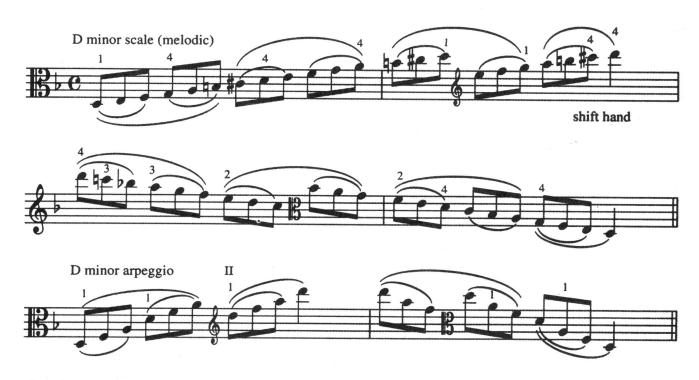

Complete Three-Octave Major and Melodic Minor Scales and Arpeggios
can be found in Suzuki Viola School Volume 7.

5 Adagio and Rondo in D

Adagio (K 356)

♩ = 72

W.A. Mozart / Preucil

p espressivo

Rondo (K 485)

W.A. Mozart / Preucil

Allegro (♩ = 132)

20

6 Hungarian Dance No.5

J. Brahms

Position Etudes

S. Suzuki

Practice these exercises on all strings

The indication  means that pupils should first play ... and then ...

The first finger should always stay down in such practice. Try stopped bows on the slurs at first.

6th Position

Also practice shifting from 2nd and 3rd fingers as shown in the following examples:

7th Position

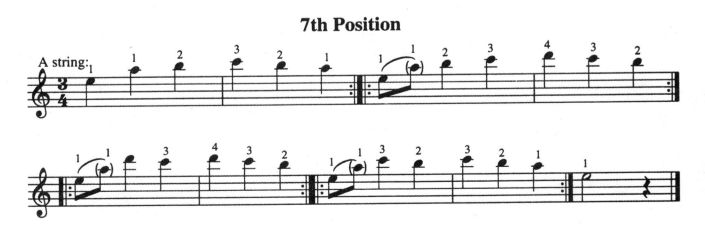

Also practice shifting from 2nd, 3rd, & 4th fingers as in example above

7 Country Dances
No. 1

Transcriptions for Viola and Pianoforte by
Watson Forbes and Alan Richardson

L. van Beethoven

VIOLA

N.B. These dances should follow
each other without a pause.

No. 2

Time of performance 5 1/2 minutes.

attacca

No. 3

No. 4

No. 5

Allegretto grazioso ♩ = 66

No. 6

Allegro molto vivace ♩ = 116

8 Concerto for Two Violins in D Minor, BWV 1043

1st movement

(Violin II arranged for Viola)*

J. S. Bach

* Violin I part can be found in Suzuki Violin School, Volume 5.

9 Concerto in C minor

J. C. Bach

Reconstituted and harmonized
by Henri Casadesus